Arduino

* * *

A Step-by-Step Guide for

Absolute Beginners

GUZZLER
MEDIA

Daniel Bell

Arduino: A Step-by-Step Guide For Absolute Beginners

Publisher: **Amazon KDP** & **Guzzler Media LLC**

http://www.guzzlermedia.com

Contact: **contact@guzzlermedia.com**

Book and Cover design by Angela W.T.

ISBN: 9781676285434

Imprint: Independently published

First Edition: December 2019

CONTENTS

Introduction

There is a high demand for electronic projects. Most electronic projects interact with the real world. The Arduino board is a great tool for one to develop hardware projects that interact with the real world. Arduino is the best platform for anyone who is beginning to program electronics. For you to load your code to the Arduino board, you are not required to have an extra hardware device. This is not the case with the previous programmable circuit boards. When using the Arduino board, you are only required to have a USB cable. This cable will allow you to connect the board to your computer. The cable will act as a pathway for loading code from your computer to the board. The same cable will also allow the Arduino board to draw charge from your computer. This means that it is not a must for you to charge the Arduino board directly from the power socket, but you can simply do it from your computer. This shows that it is easy to use the board.

The Arduino platform also uses a simplified version of the

C++ programming language. This has made it easy for beginners to learn to program. Arduino has also provided a standard form factor, breaking out the functions of the microcontroller into a package that is more accessible. The Arduino Uno is one of the versions of the Arduino boards and a great choice for beginners. The Arduino boards come with LEDs that can be programmed to light. This book is an excellent guide for you to learn how to program the Arduino board. Enjoy reading!

1-Arduino Basics

In this chapter, you will learn the basics of Arduino.

What is Arduino?

Arduino is a programmable circuit board that can be integrated into a number of simple and complex markerspace projects. The box comes with a microcontroller that can be programmed to control and sense objects in the real world. When Arduino responds to sensors and inputs, it can interact with a wide variety of outputs like motors, LEDs, and displays. Note that the board is open source. Because of the low cost and the flexibility of Arduino, it has become the best choice for makers in need of developing interactive hardware projects.

Arduino was introduced in 2005 by Massimo Banzi in Italy. The goal of introducing the board was to provide engineers with a low cost way of creating hardware projects. There are different types of Arduino boards. This difference has been brought about by the use of different microcontrollers. However, all of these boards share one thing common, which is that they are all programmed using the Arduino IDE.

Different boards have different inputs and outputs, operating voltage, speed, form factor, etc.

Board Description

In this section, we will discuss the different parts of an Arduino board:

1. The Microcontroller/ Main Chip

This is the brain of the Arduino board. This is the part which is programmed. It is the one responsible for running the code, hence it can be seen as the CPU (Central Processing Board) of the board.

This chip has some legs, which are usually plugged into the socket. These can be seen once it is taken out of the socket. However, they are not referred to as "legs" but "pins".

2. Power Jack and Supply

There are two ways on how you can supply power to your Arduino board. You may choose to use a USB connector to establish a connection to a computer or some portable power jack, or you may choose to plug it to the wall adapter. The USB can be used for powering and programming. The DC is only used for powering the board, and it is the best if you are in need of connecting the board and leaving it for some long-term project.

3. USB Jack and Interface

The USB Jack is the cable that helps you connect your board to the computer. You can use any computer, provided it has a USB port.

Some processor chips will fail when you are using a USB cable for connection to a computer. In such a case, you will have to use the serial interface. You must have a USB to the serial interface translator chip.

4. The LEDs

The Arduino comes with some lights from which you can draw ideas regarding what it is up to. The lights are referred to as LEDs. The Arduino board comes with 4 LEDs which are *L, RX, TX,* and *ON.* On the UNO board, you will find three of these at the center and one on the right side.

The ON LED will turn to green once you have powered the Arduino board. In case you find it off or flickering, then just check on your power connection.

The RX and TX boards will blink whenever data is being sent from the board or being received on the board. The TX LED will light yellow once you send data from Arduino to the computer USB port. The RX LED will light yellow whenever data is sent to Arduino from the computer's USB port.

The LED is the one that you are able to control. The other 3 LEDS usually light automatically. The L LED has been connected to the main chip of the Arduino. This can be turned on and off once you begin to write the code.

5. Headers

This is the main part of the Arduino board. These are the two lines of sockets that line up with edges of the circuit board. The thin sockets will allow you to plugin some wires into them. The wires can, in turn, be connected to any types of electronic parts including sensors, LEDs, displays, motors etc.

USB Fuse

The little USB fuse protects the computer and the Arduino. There are high chances that all types of wires will be connected to the Arduino, which may cause an accidental short on the wires. The importance of this fuse comes during this time. It is resettable, and in such occurrence, it will just open up in the same way a fuse or circuit breaker works. This will protect your board from damage.

6. Reset Button

This button is located next to the USB jack. However, on some other boards, you may find it on the right side. It is the button that can be used for restarting the Arduino. Restarting the board will only take a second, and it is done if it gets stuck or if you need to re-run some program.

7. Power up Test

We are now ready to power on our Arduino board. You can simply do this by connecting one end of your USB cable to the Arduino board and the other one to your computer. The computer will act as the source of power for the Arduino.

If you are using Arduino UNO, then the USB cable should have its end as square B-type. The USB cable should be plugged directly to the computer port. After you are sure that you are able to power the Arduino then upload the sketches, you will be set. You can then plug it to the other ports. For you to know whether the power source is working correctly, just check on whether the ON LED is lit green. The L or yellow LED may also blink or light up, which the same case with the RX and TX LEDs.

Installing the Arduino IDE

Now that you know the different parts of the Arduino board, we can learn how to prepare the Arduino IDE. After learning this, we will be ready to upload out the first program to the board. You will learn how to setup the board and set it ready to receive the program through a USB cable.

Ensure that you have the Arduino board and a USB cable. After assembling these, the next step is to download the Arduino IDE. You can download this from the following URL:

https://www.arduino.cc/en/Main/Software

Download the right version of Arduino based on the operating system that you are using. Once the download completes, unzip the downloaded file.

You can now power your board. The board can draw power from a USB connection to your computer or from an external power supply. Just connect your Arduino board to your computer via a USB cable. You should see the green power LED glow.

It is now time to launch the Arduino IDE. Open the folder where you unzipped the Arduino IDE. Double the .exe file to start the IDE.

The software will be opened and you will be able to create a new project or open an existing one. To create a new project, click File then chooses New. To open an existing project, click File, choose Example, Basics and then Blink.

You need to select the type of board that you are using. To avoid any errors when you are loading programs from the IDE to the board, ensure that you select the correct board, that is, the type of board you select in the IDE must match the type of board that is connected to your computer via the USB cable.

To select the board, click Tools then choose Board.

Next, you should select the serial port of your Arduino board. Click Tools then choose Serial Port. If you find it hard to know the serial port, just disconnect the Arduino board from the computer then look for the entry that disappears. This should be the Arduino board. You can then reconnect the board and choose that port.

Anytime you need to load a program to the Arduino board, just click the Upload button on the IDE. Note that an Arduino program is referred to as a *sketch*.

Arduino Program Structure

An Arduino program can be divided into the following three parts:

- Structure
- Values
- Functions

The Structure itself is made of two main functions:

- Setup() function
- Loop() function

These are implemented in a program as follows:

```
void setup()                    // runs
once, once the sketch starts
{
```

```
}

void loop()                          // run over
and over, or loop
{

}
```

The *setup()* function runs only once your Arduino code, commonly referred to as a *sketch* is started. It is within this function where you should initialize pin modes, variables, begin to use libraries, etc.

Once you have called the *setup()* function to initialize the initial values, the *loop()* function will loop consecutively to allow your program to respond. Use it when you need to control your Arduino function actively.

Blinkie

We will write a program that will cause an Arduino pin to blink. Just write the following code in the Arduino IDE:

```
/*
 * Blink
 *
 *A basic Arduino example.  It turns the LED
on for one second,
 * then off for one second, and this
continues
 */
int ledPin = 13;                     // LED
connected to digital pin 13

void setup()                         // run once
after the sketch is started
{
```

```
  pinMode(ledPin, OUTPUT);          // sets
digital pin as the output
}


void loop()                          // run over
and over again
{
  digitalWrite(ledPin, HIGH);     // sets LED
on
  delay(1000);                      // waits for
a second
  digitalWrite(ledPin, LOW);      // sets LED
off
  delay(1000);                      // waits for
a second
}
```

The sketch should keep on blinking the Arduino LED. The pauses between on and off should last for a second.

Arduino Comments

We use comments to explain to readers the meaning of various lines of code, making the code more understandable. The Arduino compiler will do nothing to the comments, but it will simply ignore/skip them.

To mark a single line comment in Arduino, we add // at the beginning of the line. This is demonstrated below:

```
// A single line comment in Arduino.
```

When the Arduino compiler encounters the above line, it will skip/ignore it and jump to the next line which has not been commented out.

Multi-line comments are denoted by wrapping them within /* and */. Here is an example:

```
/* A multiline comment in Arduino */
```

The Arduino Serial Library

It is possible for us to communicate from the Arduino board to the computer via a USB port. This can be done using the Serial Library.

A library refers to a collection of procedures, and all of these procedures are related. The Serial Library allows us to send data back to the computer. In serial data transfer, the transfer of data is done in terms of bits, one bit after another.

For us to pass information between the computer and the Arduino, we have to set the pin to either high or low. The technique used for switching the LED on and off can be employed to send data. Note that the size of data being transferred is measured in terms of bits and bytes. During the compilation/verification step, the sketch is always converted into binary data. Once you begin to upload the sketch to your Arduino board, it is transferred bit after a bit and then stored in the chip.

Write the sketch given below:

```
/*
 * Hello World!
 *
 * Hello World example in Arduino.
 * It demonstrates how to send data to the
board
 */
```

```
void setup()                    // run once
after the sketch starts
{
  Serial.begin(9600);           // Serial
library set up at 9600 bps

  Serial.println("Hello world");  // To
print hello
}

void loop()                     // run
again and again
{

}
```

Consider the following line extracted from the above code:

```
Serial.begin(9600);             // Serial
library set up at 9600 bps
```

This is referred to as a *library procedure call*. The name of the library is Serial, and inside this, we have a procedure named *begin()*. This statement helps us set the board with the transfer rate which is needed. This rate has been set to 9600 bits per second.

The next line in the code is as follows:

```
Serial.println("Hello world");  // To print
hello
```

This line is also calling the Serial library, and a procedure named *println* which has been defined inside that library. This is the short hand for the *print line*. The text which will be printed has been enclosed within double quotes.

You can now compile the sketch then upload it to the Arduino. You will see the sketch being launched after some seconds.

Suppose we need the Arduino to print the *Hello world* text after every second. This can be done using the following code:

```
/*
 * Hello world
 */
void setup()                          // run once
after the sketch is started
{
  Serial.begin(9600);                 // set up
the Serial library to 9600 bps
}

void loop()                           // run
again and again
{
  Serial.println("Hello world");  // prints
hello world
  delay(1000);
}
```

The code will print *Hello world* severally after each second. The *delay(1000);* statement helps us delay the Arduino for one second before printing the text.

Other than text, it is also possible for us to print out numbers. Consider the following example:

```
/*
 * Math in Arduino
 */

int x = 5;
int y = 10;
int z = 20;

void setup()                          // run once
after the sketch is started
```

```
{
  Serial.begin(9600);                    // set up a
Serial library to 9600 bps

  Serial.println("Here is the math: ");

  Serial.print("x = ");
  Serial.println(x);
  Serial.print("y = ");
  Serial.println(y);
  Serial.print("z = ");
  Serial.println(z);

  Serial.print("x + y = ");              // add
  Serial.println(x + y);

  Serial.print("x * z = ");              //
multiply
  Serial.println(x * z);

  Serial.print("z / y = ");              // divide
  Serial.println(z / y);

  Serial.print("y - z = ");              //
subtract
  Serial.println(y - z);
}

void loop()
{
}
```

You can now upload the code to the Arduino board and observe the output. You will see the numbers and the output from the various mathematical operations that we have performed in the code. Notice how we have used the *print* and *println* procedures so as to print on a single line. The latter has the new line character which moves the cursor to the next line while the former doesn't have.

Consider the following statement extracted from the code:

```
Serial.println(x);
```

The statement tells Arduino to access the value of variable x and print it. Note that this has not been enclosed within double quotes. If you ask Arduino to do the math, it can do it perfectly. The following statement adds the values of variables x and y:

```
Serial.println(x);
```

The input to the Arduino is a calculation.

Arduino has a library named *math.h* that provides us with a number of procedures that we can call to perform some complex mathematical calculations such as square root, sin, tan, etc.

Suppose we have a right angled triangle. If you are given the two sides, you can calculate the hypotenuse. Below is the formula for this:

```
h = √(x2 + y2)
```

In Arduino, the value of h can be obtained by calling the *sqrt()* function from the *math.h* library. Consider the example given below demonstrates this:

```
# include "math.h"                    // include
Math Library

int x = 3;
int y = 4;
```

```
int h;

void setup()                        // run once,
once the sketch is started
{
  Serial.begin(9600);               // set up
the Serial library to 9600 bps

  Serial.println("Calculating the value of
hypotenuse");

  Serial.print("x = ");
  Serial.println(x);

  Serial.print("y = ");
  Serial.println(y);

  h = sqrt( x*x + y*y );

  Serial.print("h = ");
  Serial.println(h);
}

void loop()                         // this is needed
even if it is empty
{
}
```

The statement *#include "math.h"* helps us instruct Arduino to include a library named *math.h* since we need to use it in the sketch. The *sqrt()* function has been defined in this library.

```
  h = sqrt( x*x + y*y );
```

The above line helps us get the sum of squares of x and y, then find their square root, and the result will be assigned to the variable *h* for the hypotenuse.

- Arduino is a programmable circuit board that can be integrated into a number of simple and complex markerspace projects.
- The box has a microcontroller that can be programmed to control and sense objects in the real world.
- The code is written in the Arduino IDE. The code is referred to as a *sketch.*
- The Arduino IDE is an open source software.
- An Arduino program is made up of two main functions, the *setup()* and *loop()* functions.
- The *setup()* function runs only once your Arduino code is started. It is within this function where you should initialize pin modes, variables, begin to use libraries, etc.
- The *loop()* function loops consecutively to allow the program to respond.

2- Arduino Data Types, Variables and Constants

In this chapter, you will learn the various data types supported in Arduino programming. We will also discuss Arduino variables.

Arduino Data Types

Data types allow us to declare variables belonging to different data types. The type of data type will determine the amount of memory space allocated to the variable and how the stored bit pattern will be interpreted.

See Arduino simply as C++ with support for libraries and some built-in assumptions that make the coding process simple. Here are the common data types in Arduino:

- Boolean- has a size of 8 bits. Takes logical values true/false.

- byte- has a size of 8 bits. It is an unsigned number with values ranging from 0-255

- char – it has a size of 8 bits. It is a signed number with values ranging from -128 to 127. The compiler tries to interpret this data type as a character in some cases, which may return unexpected results.

- unsigned char- it has a size of 8 bits. It is similar to

'byte'. This means that you can use byte if you need more clarity.

- word- has a size of 16 bits. It is an unsigned number with values ranging from 0-65535

- unsigned int- it has a size of 16 bits. It is similar to 'word'. You can use 'word' if you need more clarity and brevity.

- int- it has a size of 16 bits. It is a signed number whose values range from -32768 to 32767. It is the common data type used for general purpose variables in the Arduino example code that comes with the IDE.

- unsigned long- is has a size of 32 bits. It is an unsigned number whose values range from 0-4,294,967,295. It is commonly used to store the output of the *millis()* function, which gives the number of milliseconds for which the current code has been running.

- long- it has a size of 32 bits. It is a signed number with values ranging from -2,147,483,648 to 2,147,483,647

- float- it has a size of 32 bits. It is a signed number with values ranging from -3.4028235E38 to 3.4028235E38.

What are Variables?

A variable is a pointer to a memory location. Each variable belongs to a particular data type. The data type of the variable determines the amount of space reserved for that variable as well as the type of data that can be stored in that location.

Variable Scope

The scope is simply a section or a place within a program. The variable scope is the place within a program where a variable can be defined. It determines the places from which a variable can be accessed. In Arduino, we can define a variable in any of the following three places:

- Inside a block or a function. Such a variable is known as a *local variable.*
- Inside the definition of function parameters, known as *formal parameters.*
- Outside all functions. Such a variable is called a *global variable.*

Local Variables

A local variable is a variable that has been defined inside a block or a function. Such a variable can only be accessed and used by the statements that have been defined inside that block or function. Local variables cannot function outside their own.

The following example shows how to declare a local variable in Arduino:

```
Void setup () {

}

Void loop () {
    int a, b ;
    int c ;
    a = 0;
    b = 0;
```

```
    c = 5;
}
```

We have defined three local variables, a, b and c. Their values have been initialized thereafter. The three variables are local to the *loop()* function. Since they have been defined inside this function, they can only be accessed and used by the variables defined inside this function. Even the initialization of the variables had to be done within the same function.

Global Variables

In Arduino, global variables are defined outside all functions, at the top of the program. The global variables hold the value of variables throughout the life of the program. Since such variables are defined outside all other functions, they can be accessed from any function defined in the program. Consider the example given below:

```
Int T, S ;
float z = 0 ;

Void setup () {

}

Void loop () {
    int a, b ;
    int c ;
    a = 0;
    b = 0;
    c = 5;
}
```

In the above example, the variables T, S, and z are global variables. They have been defined outside all functions. This means that they can be accessed from within any function that is defined in the program.

However, the variables a, b and c are local to the *loop()* function. They can only be accessed by statements that have been defined inside this function.

- A variable points to a memory location for storage of values.
- A variable must belong to a particular data type. The value of a variable can be changed.
- The name of a variable can only have letters, digits and an underscore. It must start with either a letter or an underscore.
- The scope of a variable is determined by the place of the definition of the variable within the sketch.
- The scope of a variable determines the place within the sketch from where the variable can be accessed.
- A local variable is a variable defined within a function. It can only be accessed from within that function.
- A global variable is a variable defined outside all functions. It can be accessed from anywhere within the program.

3-Arduino Operators

In this chapter, you will learn the various operators supported in Arduino.

An operator is simply a symbol that instructs the compiler to perform a particular mathematical or logical operation. We can use an operator to check, change or even combine values. Examples of operators are the addition operator (+) that adds two numbers and the AND operator (&&) that combines two values of a Boolean type.

Let us discuss the various operators that you can use in Arduino:

Arithmetic Operators

These operators are used to perform standard mathematical operations on the operands. Arduino supports the following arithmetic operators:

- Addition Operator (+)- for adding two operands.
- Subtraction Operator (-)- for subtracting the second operand from the first operand.
- Multiplication Operator (*)- multiplies both operands.
- Division Operator (/)- divides the numerator by the denominator.
- Modulo operator (%)- returns the remainder after

division.

The following example demonstrates how to use these types of operators:

```
void loop () {
    int x = 7, y = 2, result;
    result = x + y;
    result = x - y;
    result = x * y;
    result = x / y;
    result = x % y;
}
```

We have declared three variables, *x, y,* and *result*. The variables x and y hold the values of the operands, while the variable *result* will hold the result of each arithmetic operation. The code should return the following:

```
x + y = 9
x - y = 5
x * y = 14
x / y = 3.5
Remainder when x divided by y = 1
```

Comparison Operators

These types of operators are used to make comparisons between values. They are applied to two operands. Arduino supports the standard comparison operators that are supported in the C programming language. They include the following:

- Equal to the operator (==)- checks whether the values of two operands are equal or not. If the two are equal, the operator returns a TRUE.

- Not equal to the operator (!=)- checks whether the values of the two operators are equal or not. It becomes TRUE if the values of the operands are not equal.

- Greater than operator (>)- checks whether the value of the left operand is greater than the value of the right operand. If yes, the operator returns a TRUE.

- Less than operator (<)-checks whether the value of the left operand is less than the value of the right operand. If yes, the operator returns a TRUE.

- Greater than or equal to the operator (>=)-checks whether the value of the left operand is greater than or equal to the value of the right operand. If yes, the operator returns a TRUE.

- Less than or equal to the operator (<=)-checks whether the value of the left operand is less than or equal to the value of the right operand. If yes, the operator returns a TRUE.

Consider the example given below:

```
void loop () {
    int x = 7, y = 2
    bool result = false;
    if(x == y)
        result = true;
    else
        result = false;

    if(x != y)
        result = true;
    else
        result = false;

    if(x < y)
```

```
      result = true;
   else
      result = false;

   if(x > y)
      result = true;
   else
      result = false;

   if(x <= y)
      result = true;
   else
      result = false;

   if(x >= y)
      result = true;
   else
      result = false;
}
```

We have declared three variables, *x, y,* and *result*. The variables x and y hold the values of the operands, while the variable *result* will hold the result of each comparison operation. Note that the *result* is a Boolean variable, meaning that it can take a value of either *true* or *false*. The code should return the following:

```
result = false
result = true
result = false
result = true
result = false
result = false
```

The value of x was initialized to 7 while that of y was initialized to 2. The operations have then been performed on these two values to return the above.

Boolean Operators

These operators are used to perform logical operations on operands. They include the following:

- Logical AND operator (&&) - Becomes TRUE when the operands are non-zero.

- Logical OR operator (||) - Becomes TRUE when one of the operands is non-zero.

- Logical NOT operator (!) - It reverses the logical state of an operand.

For example:

```
void loop () {
    int x = 7, y = 2
    bool result = false;
    if((x > y)&& (y < x))
     result    = true;
    else
       result = false;

    if((x == y)|| (y < x))
       result = true;
    else
       result = false;

    if( !(x == y)&& (y < x))
       result = true;
    else
       result = false;
}
```

The code will return the following:

```
result = true
result = true
result = true
```

In the first operation, we are using the && Boolean operator. Both parts returned true, hence, *true&&true* is true.

In our second operation, we are using the || Boolean operator. The first part evaluated to a false, while the second part evaluated to a true. Hence, *false||true* returns a *true*.

In the last operation, we are using two Boolean operators, ! and &&. The first operation, x==y, will evaluate to a false. The second operation, y<x, will evaluate to a true. When the && operator is applied, false&&true will return a *false*. The ! operator was then applied as *!false*, which returned *true*.

- Arduino supports various types of operators. These are the same operators that are supported in C.
- Arithmetic operators help us perform various arithmetic/mathematical operations in Arduino.
- Comparison operators are used to performing comparison operations between the values of operands.
- Boolean operators help in performing logical operations on operands.

4-Control Statements

In this chapter, we will discuss the various decision making statements supported in Arduino.

In decision making, we specify a condition or a set of conditions that are to be evaluated alongside the actions to be taken based on the outcome of the evaluation. The evaluation of the condition normally involves checking whether the condition is true or false. If true, a particular action is taken, if false, another action may be taken or nothing may be done.

Arduino supports a number of statements that we can use for decision making. These will form the center of discussion in this chapter.

if Statement

This is a control flow statement used when we need to perform a set of different actions based on specified conditions that are either true or false. The statement takes the syntax given below:

```
if (expression) {
    // statement(s)
}
```

The *expression* in the above syntax is simply the condition to be evaluated. If the condition is true, the statement(s) placed within the body of the *if* statement {} will be executed, otherwise, execution will jump to the first statement immediately after the body of the if, that is, after the closing curly brace }.

For example:

```
/* Defining global variables */
int X = 2 ;
int Y = 7 ;

Void setup () {

}

Void loop () {
    /* checking boolean condition */
    if (X > Y) /* if condition is true,
execute the following statement*/
    X++;
    /* checking boolean condition */
    If ( ( X < Y ) && ( Y != 0 )) /* if
condition is true, execute the following
statement*/ {
        X += Y;
```

```
        Y--;
    }
}
```

We first created two global variables, X and Y. There values were initialized to 2 and 7 respectively. In the first, *if* statement, we are checking whether the value of variable X is greater than the value of variable Y. This is false, hence, the statement below this will not be executed. The expression in the second *if* statement will evaluate into a true because X is less than Y and Y is not equal to 0. The statements below this will be executed.

The expression *X += Y* will add the values of X and Y and assign the result to the variable X, hence, the new value of X will become 9. The expression Y- - will decrease the value of Y by 1, hence, the new value of Y will become 6.

if... else Statement

This Arduino statement is made up of two statements, the *if* statement and the *else* statement. We use this statement when we need to specify the part that will be executed when the *if* the condition evaluates to a false. This is specified within the *else* part. It takes the syntax given below:

```
if(expression) {
    // statement(s) to be executed if the
Boolean expression is true
} else {
    // statement(s) to be executed if the
Boolean expression is false
}
```

For example:

```
/* Defining a global variable */
int X = 2 ;
int Y = 7 ;

Void setup () {

}

Void loop () {
    /* checking the boolean condition */
    if (X > Y) /* if condition is true,
execute the following statement*/ {
        X++;
    }else {
        Y -= X;
    }
}
```

We defined two global variables, X and Y, and assigned them values 2 and 7 respectively. In the *if* condition, we are checking whether the value of X is greater than Y, which is false. This means that the statement below the *if* statement will not be executed. The Arduino compiler will then jump to execute the *else* part. S*tatement Y -=X* will be executed. The value of X will be extracted from the value of Y and the result assigned to the variable Y. The new value of the variable will then become 5.

if... else if ... else statement

This statement should be used when there is a need to test multiple conditions. In this statement, you should begin by a single *if* statement, followed by any number of *else if* statements and lastly an *else* statement. The last statement, that is, *else* will be executed when none of the previous conditions have evaluated to a true. This syntax is given below:

```
if(expression 1) {
   // Executes when the expression 1 is true
} else if(expression 2) {
   // Executes when the expression 2 is true
} else if(expression 3) {
   // Executes when the expression 3 is true
} else {
   // executes when none of the above
conditions is true.
}
```

For example:

```
/* Defining a global variable */
int X = 2 ;
int Y = 7 ;
int z = 13;

Void setup () {

}

Void loop () {
   /* checking the Boolean condition */
   if (X > Y) /* if condition is true,
execute the following statement*/ {
      X++;
   }
   /* checking the Boolean condition */
   else if ((X == Y )||( Y < z) ) /* if
condition is true,
      execute the following statement*/ {
      z = Y* X;
   }else
      z++;
}
```

In the above example, we first created three global variables, X, Y, and z and initialized their values to 2, 9 and 13 respectively. In the *if* statement, we are checking whether the value of x is greater than the value of Y, which is false. This means that the statement below it, that is, X++, will not be executed. In the *else, if* statement, the whole expression will evaluate to a true because of the use of the || operator. The first part, X==Y, will evaluate to a false. The second part, Y<z, will evaluate to a true. false||true gives a true, hence, the statement below this expression will be executed. The values of X and Y will be multiplied to give the new value of z, which is 14. The execution of the program will halt there.

switch case Statement

Sometimes, we may have a very long *if..else...if* statement. The *switch case* statement acts as a substitute for this, especially when the pattern under evaluation is complex. It uses a number of *case* statements for performing different actions based on various conditions. It simply compares the value specified in the *switch* statement with the values specified using the *case* statements.

The *switch case* statement stops execution immediately a matching *case* is found, meaning that the rest of the cases will not be evaluated. Here is the syntax for the *switch* statement:

```
switch(variable){
case value_1:
 //code for execution;
 break;
case value_2:
 //code for execution;
```

```
break;
......
```

```
default:
 //code for execution if no case is matched;
 break;
}
```

The switch statement will get the value of the variable/expression at the top, then begin to compare it with the various cases. Once a case is matched, the statement within the case will be executed and the switch statement will halt the execution. The cases are executed from the top to the bottom, and when a case is not matched, the compiler will proceed to the next one. If none of all the cases are matched, the *default* part will be executed.

Let us create an example to demonstrate this:

Suppose we have a variable named *state* which can only take three possible states, 0, 1 and 3. There are three functions, each corresponding to each of these three states. This can be implemented using a *switch case* statement as shown below:

```
switch (state) {
   case 0: Low();
break;
   case 1: Mid();
break;
   case 2: Hig();
break;
   default: Message("Unknown state!");
}
```

When the value of the *state* variable is 0, the function *Low()* will be called. When the value of the variable 1, the function *Mid()*

will be called. When the value of the variable is 2, the function *Hig()* will be called. This means that the function to be called will be determined by the case whose value is matched with the value of the *state* variable.

- Decision making helps us evaluate conditions and take actions based on the outcome of the evaluation.
- The *if* statement helps us evaluate a condition and take action if the evaluation becomes true.
- With the *if...else* statement, the *if* statement is executed if the condition is true while the *else* statement is executed if the condition is false.
- In the *if...else...if* statement, we can test many conditions and take action based on the true conditions.
- The *switch* statement makes it simple for us when we have multiple *else if* statements. The *switch* statement gets the value of a variable/expression and tries to compare it with other values specified using *case* to find a match.

5- Arduino Loops

In this chapter, we will be discussing the various loop control statements supported in Arduino.

Loops provide us with an automated way of performing certain tasks repetitively. This is the case when we need to execute part of our code repeatedly. The statements of code placed within a loop are executed sequentially, that is, in the order that you have written them. The loop will execute the statements from the first to the second etc.

Here are the various loop statements supported in Arduino:

while Loop

The *while* loop will execute a statement or a set of statements as long as the provided condition is true. The loop will halt execution immediately the condition becomes false. The *while* loop takes the syntax given below:

```
while (test_expression) {
    // statement(s)
}
```

If the *test_expression* is true, the statement(s) within the body of the *while* loop will be executed. The *text_expression* will be evaluated before each iteration. When it becomes false, the execution of the statement(s) will stop.

Consider the example given below:

```
void setup() {
int x = 0;
while (x < 10) {
  // repeat 10 times
 Serial.println(x);
  x++;
    }
}
void loop(){
}
```

In the above example, we have created a variable named *x* and initialized its value to 0. In the text expression placed inside the *while* loop, we are checking for whether the value of x is less than 10. If this is true, the statements placed within the body of the *while* will be executed. These will just print the values of x from 0 to 9.

Note that 10 is not part of the output. This is because we use the less than symbol (<) symbol, meaning that the value of x must be less than 10. The moment the Arduino compiler finds the value of x is 10, it will stop execution immediately to avoid violating the *while* condition.

Consider the following line of the code:

```
Serial.println(x);
```

This line will print the value of the variable x on the serial monitor window.

do...while Loop

In the *while l*oop, we were evaluating the loop control condition at the top of the loop body. Due to this, we may have some cases were the body of the loop wuill never be executed. A good example is when the *test_expression* of the loop evaluates to a false on the first test.

This is different from the *do...while* loop. The loop control condition is evaluated at the end of the loop body. This means that the loop body must be evaluated for at least once, even when the condition evaluates to a false for the first time. This type of loop takes the following syntax:

```
do {
    statement(s);
}
while( condition );
```

After the first iteration, when the condition evaluates to a true, control will jump back to the do part. If it evaluates to a false, the execution will continue downwards without going back to the loop. This means that as long as the condition is true, the loop body will keep on executing. Let us create an example that demonstrates this:

```
void setup() {
    int sum = 0;

    Serial.begin(9600);

    do {
        sum = sum + 10;
        Serial.print("sum = ");
        Serial.println(sum);
        delay(500);                        // a delay of
500 milliseconds
```

```
    } while (sum < 50);
}

void loop() {
}
```

In the above example, we have declared an integer *sum* and initialized its value to a 0. We have then created a *do…while* loop. The test condition in the above example comes at the end of the loop body. This means that before this is evaluated, the body of the loop will have been executed once. In the first pass, the code will print a 10 as the value of the variable *sum*. The condition *x<50* will then be evaluated and found to be true. The loop will then jump to the *do* and execute the loop body again to return a 20. Note that the statement *sum = sum + 10* will increase the value of the variable *sum* by 10 after every iteration. This will continue until the loop finds itself violating the condition *sum<50*. This is when the execution of the loop will halt.

for Loop

This type of loop is good and efficient when you know the exact number of times that you need to repeat a task. The loop takes the following syntax:

```
for ( initial; condition; increment ) {
    statement(s);
}
```

The *initial* part of the loop allows you to declare and initialize the variable that you will use to control the execution of the loop. For example, we can use a variable x. We can set it to *x=5*.

The *condition* part is where you specify the condition that must be true for the loop body to be executed. In our case, this is where we specify that the value of variable x should be less than or equal to 10. We can set this to x<=10.

The *increment* is where the flow will jump after every iteration. It specifies how we should modify the loop control variable after every iteration. This is where we add the x++ statement to increment the variable by 1 after every iteration.

The compiler will evaluate the condition after every iteration to check whether it is true or false. If true, it will jump to the increment part then the loop body. This is repeated until the condition becomes false.

Here is an example:

```
void setup (void) {

    Serial.begin(9600);

    for (int x=0; x<10; x++)
        Serial.println(x);
}

void loop(void) {
}
```

The code will print the values of x from o to 9. We created a variable x and initialized its values to a 0. In the loop condition, we have specified that the value of x should be less than 10. The increment increases the value of x by 1 after every iteration. When the loop finds itself violating the loop condition, that is, x<10, it will stop the execution. That is why the code will return the values of x from 0 to 10.

Nested for Loop

We get a nested *for* loop when we add a *for* loop inside another *for* loop. For a single iteration of the outer loop, the inner loop will be executed fully. This means that if the outer loop is executed for 4 times, the inner loop will be executed 4 times for each, meaning that it will be executed 16 times.

A nested *for* loop takes the following syntax:

```
for (initial; condition; increment) {
    // statement (s)
    for (initial; condition; increment) {
        // statement (s)
    }
}
```

Consider the example given below:

```
void setup (void) {

    Serial.begin(9600);

for(x = 0; x<= 4; x ++) {
    //statements will executed 5 times
    for(y = 0; y<= 9; y++) {
        //statements will executed 10 times
    }
}
}

void loop(void) {
}
```

In the outer *for* loop, we have initialized the variable x. In the inner *for* loop, we have initialized the variable *y*. For a single execution of the outer *for* loop, the inner *for* loop will run 10 times. Since the outer *for* loop will run for 5 times, the inner *for* loop will run for 50 times.

infinite Loop

This is a type of loop that will run forever. It does not have a terminating condition. An infinite loop can be implemented in a *for* loop, *while* loop or the *do...while* loop. All we need to do in these loops is to remove the loop control condition. The purpose of this condition is to state the circumstances under which should run and when it should halt the execution. When removed, we will not have a way of stating when the loop should stop the execution, hence, the loop will run forever.

The following example demonstrates how to create an infinite loop with the *for* loop:

```
void setup (void) {
    Serial.begin(9600);
    for (;;) {
      Serial.print("Hello World");
}
}

void loop(void) {
}
```

When executed, the above loop will run forever. For each iteration, it will print *Hello World*.

The following example demonstrates how to create an infinite loop using the *while* loop:

```
void setup (void) {
    Serial.begin(9600);
    while (1) {
```

```
    Serial.print("Hello World");
}
}

void loop(void) {
}
```

The code will print the *Hello World* statement forever. Instead of adding the condition inside the *while* loop, we only added a 1. This will always evaluate to a true, hence, the loop will run forever.

The following example demonstrates how to create an infinite loop using the *do...while* loop:

```
void setup (void) {
    Serial.begin(9600);
 do {
        Serial.print("Hello World");
}
while(1);
}
void loop(void) {
}
```

In the text condition, we have added a 1. This will always evaluate to a true, hence, the loop will print the statement *Hello World* forever.

- Arduino loops help us perform a set of tasks repetitively.
- The *for* loop can be used to iterate over a statement(s) over a fixed number of times.
- The *while* loop executes a task repetitively as long as a particular condition is true.
- The *do...while* loop must be executed for at least once,

whether the test condition is true or false.

- Loop control statements help us alter the normal execution of a program.
- We can create infinite loops, which are loops that run forever.
- Infinite loops run forever because they lack a loop control condition.

6- Arduino Functions

In this chapter, you will learn the use and various features of Arduino functions.

What is a Function?

A function refers to a set of statements that perform related tasks. Other than the *setup()* and the *loop()* functions in Arduino, it is possible for more functions to be defined within a program.

An Arduino program can be subdivided into a set of functions. The way you sub-divide the code lies up to you, but it should be done in such a way that every function performs a certain task.

When such code is grouped together and given a name, it becomes easy for you to reuse the code by calling and calling it again using the function name. Again, the code will become optimized since there will be no need for you to write it again. Suppose your goal is to check three numbers, 150, 230 and 450 to tell whether they are even or not. Without the use of a function, you will have to write the logic for the even number each time. This will be a repetition of code. However, by use of a function, you can write the logic only once and keep on calling it.

When creating a function in an Arduino program, make sure that it lies outside the brackets of the *setup()* and the *loop()* functions.

Function Declaration

The work of a function declaration is to tell the Arduino compiler about the name of the function, its return type, and parameters. The function should be declared outside the two functions, that is, *setup()* and *loop()* functions, either at the top or at the bottom. To define a function in Arduino, we use the following syntax:

```
returnType functionName(argument1,
argument2, …)
{
//function body code
}
```

A function can return any value. The *returnType* denotes the data type of the value returned by the function. However, there are functions that will perform their tasks without returning values. In such a case, the return type should be *void*.

The *functionName* is the name of the function. The functionName together with the parameter list form the function signature.

See an argument as a *placeholder*. When you invoke a function, you pass a value to the argument. The value will be the actual parameter or argument. Note that each parameter is associated with a data type. Also, note that there are functions without arguments. The function body should have statements defining what the function should when invoked.

The following example demonstrates how to define a function in Arduino:

```
int sum (int a, int b) // function
declaration {
    int c = 0;
    c = a+b ;
    return c; // return the value
}

void setup () {
    Statement(s)
}

Void loop () {
    }
```

Above, we have defined a function named *sum()* that takes in two integer parameters, a and b. The function will add together the values of these two parameters and assign the result to the variable c. We could also have defined the function as follows:

```
int sum (int , int ) ; // function prototype

void setup () {
    Statement(s)
}

Void loop () {
    }

int sum (int a, int b) // function
declaration {
    int c = 0;
    c = a+b ;
    return c; // return the value
}
```

In the second method, the function was declared just above the loop function.

Function Call

Defining a function is not enough. Defining a function helps us declare what it should do. We do not need it to perform a task. This can be achieved by calling the function. It is after the function call that the function does its work and returns the expected value.

We pass the values of the parameters when calling or invoking the function. The arguments are then copied to the parameters for the function to operate on them. A function is called by its name. The values of the parameters are then passed inside in the order by which they were defined. The call to the function should be done within the *loop()* function as shown below:

```
int sum (int a, int b) // function
declaration {
    int c = 0;
    c = a+b ;
    return c; // return the value
}

void setup () {
    Statement(s)
}

Void loop () {
    int result = 0 ;
    result = sum (4,8) ; // function call
    Serial.println(result);
}
```

The code will print 12 upon execution. When calling the function within the *loop()* function, we have passed 4,8 to the name of the function, that is, *sum*. From the definition of the function, it should add the values of the two parameters, a and b. The 4 will become the value of parameter *a* while the 8 will become the value of parameter *b*. These two will be added to return a 12.

In the second method of defining the function, we could have called it as follows:

```
int sum (int , int ) ; // function prototype

void setup () {
    Statement(s)
}

Void loop () {
    int result = 0 ;
    result = sum (4, 8) ; // function call
}

int sum (int a, int b) // function
declaration {
    int c = 0;
    c = a+b ;
    return c; // return the value
}
```

Again, the call to the function was done within the *loop()* function.

Here is another example:

```
void setup(){
    Serial.begin(9600);
}

void loop() {
    int x = 4;
    int y = 3;
    int z;
```

```
  z = multiplyFunction(x, y); // z now
contains 12
  Serial.println(z);
  delay(500);
}

int multiplyFunction(int a, int b){
  int result;
  result = a * b;
  return result;
}
```

The code will print 12 when executed. We began by defining three integer variables, x, y, and z. The variables x and y were assigned values of 4 and 3 respectively. The variable z has been assigned the value that is returned by a function named *multiplyFunction()*. This is the value that should be printed as shown in the call to the *println()* function.

In the last section of the program, we have defined what the *multiplyFunction()* should. The function takes two integer parameters, *a* and *b* and multiplies their values. The output of this should be assigned to the variable *result*.

- Arduino function groups together code that is intended to perform a similar or related task.

- To call a function, we use its name and pass the arguments to it. The function will return the expected result.

- In Arduino, functions should be defined outside the *setup()* and the *loop()* functions.

- The definition of the function can be done above or below the above two functions.

7- Arduino Arrays

Arrays are used for the storage of many values that belong to the same data type. The elements should all be either integers, strings, doubles etc. See an array as a container for storing many values that belong to the same data type in an ordered manner. When the elements are fetched from the array, they should be returned in the same order that they were added into the array.

An array is defined by a name. The elements of the array are accessed by their position. The position of each element is referred to as an *index*. This means that we also access the elements using their indexes. The first element in the array is said to be at index 0 of the array while the last element is said to be at index n-1, where n is the total number of elements in the array.

Declaring an Array

With an array, you don't have to declare all the variables. What you do is that you declare a single array and give it a name. You can then store the ages of different individuals into that array.

Array declaration in Arduino involves telling the Arduino compiler the data type of the array elements, the array name and the number of elements to be stored in the array. An array is declared using the following syntax:

```
type array_Name [ arraySize ];
```

That is how we declare one-dimensional arrays in Arduino. The *type* can be any valid Arduino data type, the *array_Name* is the name you assign to the array while the *arraySize* is the number of elements you want to store in the array, and this must be an integer constant with a value greater than 0. For example:

To create an array named *age* to store 10 elements, we can use the following statement:

```
int age[ 11 ];
```

We have declared an array named *age* to store 20 integers. The compiler will reserve the right amount of memory for this.

Assign Values to an Array

An array is used for storage of data. There are different ways through which we can add values into an array. The position of each element is denoted using an index, written inside square brackets []. For example:

```
an_array[0] = 12;    // assign a value of
12 to the 1st element
an_array[1] = 11;  // assign a value of 11
to the 2nd element, etc.
an_array[2] = 9;
an_array[3] = 14;
an_array[4] = 97;
```

In the above example, we have used array indexes to state the elements that should be stored in the respective indexes of the array named *an_array*. The element 12 will be stored at index 0, 11 at index 1, 9 at index 2, 14 at index 3 and 97 at index 4.

The initialization could also have been done in a single line as follows:

```
int an_array[5] = {12, 11, 9, 14, 97};
```

The elements will be added to the array in the order that you have used to specify them. The value 12 will be stored at the index 0 of the array, the value 11 at index 1 of the array, the value 9 at index 2 of the array, etc.

We can use a *for* loop to add values to an array. This requires us to create a loop variable that will iterate over the various indexes of the array. For example:

```
int n[ 10 ] ; // n is an array of 10
integers
void setup () {

}

void loop () {
    for ( int p = 0; p < 10; ++p ){//
initialize array elements n to 0
        n[ p ] = 0; // set element at location
p to 0
        Serial.print(p) ;
        Serial.print('\r') ;
    }
```

In the above example, we have created the variable *p* as the loop variable. The *for* loop will create values 0 to 9, which will form the indexes of the array. At each iteration, a value of 0 will be assigned to each index of the array. This means that the array will store 10 0s.

Accessing Array Values

To access an element of an array, we only have to index the array. We only have to place the index at which the element is located within square brackets after the array name. The simplest way to access the elements of an array is by creating a *for* loop. We can use the loop to iterate over the elements of the array. For example:

```
for (x = 0; x < 5; x++) {
    Serial.println(an_array[x]);
  }
```

In the above example, we have created a *for* loop and a loop variable named *x*. The values of the variable will range between 0 and 4. The statement *an_array[x]* has then been used to access the values of the array at various indexes. In the first iteration, this will return the value stored at index 0 of the array *an_array*. In the second iteration, this will return the value stored at index 1 of array *an_array*, and this continues. These values will then be printed on the serial monitor window.

Using Arrays

Consider the example given below:

```
int n[ 10 ] ; // n is an array of 10
integers

void setup () {

}

void loop () {
   for ( int p = 0; p < 10; ++p ){//
initialize array elements n to 0
      n[ p ] = 0; // set element at location
p to 0
      Serial.print(p) ;
      Serial.print('\r') ;
   }
   for ( int q = 0; q < 10; ++q ){ // output
each array element's value {
      Serial.print(n[q]) ;
      Serial.print('\r') ;
   }
}
```

In the above example, we have created an array named *n* to store a list of 10 integers. We have then used two *for* loops inside the *loop()* function. Inside the first *for* loop, we have created the variable *p*. This is the variable that we have used to iterate over the indexes of the array. This loop has been used to initialize the elements of the array *n*. It will create the 10 indexes of the array marking the positions where we should store the various elements.

Consider the following line extracted from the code:

```
n[ p ] = 0;
```

The above line will initialize the values at all array indexes to 0. This means that the array will store 10 0s, right from index 0 to index 9. Consider the following line extracted from the code:

```
Serial.print(p) ;
```

This will print all the indexes of the array from 0 to 9 on the serial monitor window.

In the second loop, we have created the variable *q*. This variable will be used to iterate over all the array indexes, right from index 0 to index 9. Consider the following line extracted from the code:

```
Serial.print(n[q]) ;
```

The *n[q]* will print the element stored in the index array *q* of the array *n* on the serial monitor window. This will happen after every iteration. Since the array holds elements 0 from index 0 to 9, this line will print a 0 after every iteration. At the end of it, it will return 10 0s.

Consider the next example given below:

```
void setup() {
   int an_array[5] = {12, 11, 9, 14, 97};
   int x;

   Serial.begin(9600);

   // display each array value on the serial
monitor window
   for (x = 0; x < 5; x++) {
     Serial.println(an_array[x]);
   }
}
void loop() {
```

```
}
```

In the above example, we have created an array named *an_array*. This array is storing a list of 5 integers. The initialization of the array elements was done in the following line:

```
int an_array[5] = {12, 11, 9, 14, 97};
```

We have then used the variable *x* to iterate through the elements of the array. At each iteration, the code will print will print the value stored at a particular index of the array. The code will return all the 5 integers stored in the array. Consider the next example given below:

```
void setup() {
  int an_array[5];       // an array to store
5 integer elements
  int x;

  Serial.begin(9600);

  an_array[0] = 12;      // assign a value of
12 to the 1st element
  an_array[1] = 11;  // assign a value of 11
to the 2nd element, etc.
  an_array[2] = 9;
  an_array[3] = 14;
  an_array[4] = 97;

  // display each array element in the
serial monitor window
  for (x = 0; x < 5; x++) {
    Serial.println(an_array[x]);
  }
}
void loop() {
}
```

We began by creating an array named *an_array* to store 5 integers. We have then created an integer variable *x* that we will use to iterate through the elements of the array. This time, we have manually assigned elements to the array. Consider the following line extracted from the code:

```
an_array[0] = 12;
```

The above line simply tells the Arduino compiler to store the number 12 in index 0 of the array named *an_array*. This means that 12 will be the first value of the array named *an_array*. This has been done up to index 4 of the array since it will store only 5 elements. We have then used a *for* loop and the variable *x* to iterate over the elements of the array and print them on the serial monitor window.

Modifying Array Elements

To change the value of an array, we can use the assignment operator. If it is about changing the value of an array, we have to specify the index of the value and the new value that should be stored in that index. Of course, the index should be specified in square brackets []. For example:

```
an_array[0] = 10;
```

In the above example, we are changing the value stored at index 0 of an array named *an_array* to 10. This means that the new value of at index 0 of the array will become 10.

- An array is a data structure that stores elements of the same data type.
- The elements of an array are stored sequentially.
- The elements are also accessed sequentially.
- The elements of an array can be changed, but the array size cannot be changed.
- We can use the *for* loop to iterate over the array elements.

8- Arduino Strings

Strings are used for the storage of text. It can be used for the display of text on the Arduino IDE Serial Monitor window or on an LCD. We can also use Strings to store input received from users. A good example is the characters typed by a user on a keyboard that has been connected to the Arduino.

There are two types of strings in Arduino programming:

- Arrays of characters. These are similar to the strings that are used in the C programming language.
- Arduino String. This is the type of string object that can be used in an Arduino sketch.

String Character Arrays

This is a type of string that is simply made up of a series of characters that belong to the *char* data type. As we stated previously, an array is a data structure that stores elements of the same data type. See a string as an array of char variables.

A string is a special array with one extra element at the end of the string, whose value is always a zero (0). This is called a "null terminated string." Here is an example that shows how we can create a string and display it on the serial monitor window:

```
void setup() {
  char my_string[6]; // an array to hold a
5 character string
```

```
    Serial.begin(9600);
    my_string[0] = 'S'; // the string has 5
characters
    my_string[1] = 'a';
    my_string[2] = 'm';
    my_string[3] = 'm';
    my_string[4] = 'y';
    my_string[5] = 0; // the 6th element is a
null terminator
    Serial.println(my_string);
}
void loop() {
}
```

The above example shows what a string is made up of, a set of printable characters and a 0 at the end. The purpose of the 0 is to show the end of the string. The string can be printed on the serial monitor window by calling the *Serial.println()* function. See that the first character of the string is an index 0 of the string.

The same string can also be written more conveniently as shown below:

```
void setup() {
    char my_string[] = "Sammy";
    Serial.begin(9600);
    Serial.println(my_string);
}
void loop() {
}
```

The compiler will calculate the size of the string array and then null terminate it automatically with a zero. This will create a 6-elements long array of five characters followed by a zero.

Manipulating String Arrays

We can create an Arduino sketch and use it to alter a string array. Consider the example given below:

```
void setup() {
   char my_string[] = "I love coffee and
cake"; // create a string
   Serial.begin(9600);
   // print out the string
   Serial.println(my_string);
   // delete a section of the  string
   my_string[13] = 0;
   Serial.println(my_string);
   // substitute a word in the string
   my_string[13] = ' '; // replace the null
terminator with space
   my_string[18] = 't'; // insert a new word
   my_string[19] = 'e';
   my_string[20] = 'a';
   my_string[21] = 0; // terminate the
string
   Serial.println(my_string);
}

void loop() {
}
```

In the above example, we have created a string named *my_string*. We have then called *Serial.println()* function so as to print the string on the serial monitor window. This will print the whole string as follows:

```
I love coffee and cake
```

Next, we have deleted a section of the string. The deletion will begin from index 13 of the string. This has been achieved by the following line:

```
my_string[13] = 0;
```

The above line tells the compiler the section of the string *my_string* from index 13. This will delete the *"and cake"* part of the string. Now, when we print the string, it will return the following:

```
I love coffee
```

We now have a new string. Consider the following line extracted from the code:

```
my_string[13] = ' ';
```

We are trying to insert a new space so that we can insert a new word at the end of the sentence. We have replaced the null terminator of the string with space.

It is after this that we have inserted the word *tea* into the string. This has been done from index 13 of the string. This will return the following:

```
I love coffee and tea
```

Note that the index 13 denotes the 14th character of the string. We shortened the string by replacing this character with a null terminating zero. This is the element at number 13 of the string when we count from 0.

When we printed the string, it returned all characters up to the new null terminating zero. Note that the rest of the characters do not disappear, but they are still kept in the computer memory. This means that the length of the string is still the same. The difference is brought by the fact that any function working with the string will only be able to see the string up to the position of the first null terminator.

In the sketch, the word cake was replaced with the word *tea*. Remember we had inserted a null terminator at position 13. We had to replace this will space so that we can have our string formatted as it was originally. This is normally done by overwriting individual characters. The result is normally that the string is actually terminated with two null characters, the original one at the end of the string then a new one to replace the 'e' in the word "cake". This will make no difference when the new string has been printed since the function that prints the string will stop printing the string characters after it encounters the first null terminator. Overall, the sketch should return the following output:

```
I like coffee and cake
I like coffee
I like coffee and tea
```

String Manipulation Functions

In the previous example, we manipulated the string in a manual way. We had to access the individual characters of the string using their respective indexes. However, you can create your own functions and use them to manipulate the strings. This will make the task of manipulating strings easy for you. Some of these functions are borrowed from the C language library.

The following example demonstrates how we can use some functions from the C language library to manipulate strings:

```
void setup() {
   char my_string[] = "This is my string"; // create a string
   char outer_str[40]; // result from the string functions stored here
   int x; // a general purpose integer
   Serial.begin(9600);

   // print the string
   Serial.println(my_string);

   // get the string length, excluding the null terminator
   x = strlen(my_string);
   Serial.print("String length is: ");
   Serial.println(x);

   // get the array length, including null terminator
   x = sizeof(my_string); // sizeof() is not a C string function
   Serial.print("Size of the array: ");
   Serial.println(x);

   // copy a string
   strcpy(outer_str, my_string);
   Serial.println(outer_str);

   // add a string to the end of a string (append)
   strcat(outer_str, " sketch.");
   Serial.println(outer_str);
   x = strlen(outer_str);
   Serial.print("String length is: ");
   Serial.println(x);
   x = sizeof(outer_str);
```

```
    Serial.print("Size of the array
outer_str[]: ");
    Serial.println(x);
}

void loop() {
}
```

The code should return the following upon execution:

```
This is my string
String length is: 17
Size of the array: 18
This is my string
This is my string sketch.
String length is: 25
Size of the array outer_str[]: 40
```

We began by creating a string. This string was given the name *my_string*. This string was then printed on the serial monitor window.

To know the length of a string, use the *strlen()* function as we have done above. The string length is only determined by the printable characters and the null terminator is not included. Our string has a total of 17 characters, and 17 characters were printed on the serial monitor window.

The *sizeof()* operator helped us get the length of the array that holds the string. This length will include the null terminator, meaning that it will be one length more than the length of the string.

The *sizeof()* looks more like a function, but it is simply an operator. It is not included in the C string library. We used it to show that there is a difference between the size of the array and the size of the string.

The *strcpy()* function was used to copy the string named *my_string[]* to the variable *outer_str[]* array. The *strcpy()* function will copy the second string passed to it into the first string. The *outer_num[]* array now has a copy of the string, but it only takes 18 elements of the array. This means that the array still has 22 free char elements. The elements will be found in the memory after the string.

The propose of copying the string to the array was so that we could have some extra space in the array to be used in the next part of the sketch, in which we will be adding a new string to the end of the string.

We have also used the sketch to join a string to another string. This process is known as *concatenation*. We have used the *strcat()* function for this. This function works by adding the second string that has been passed to it to the end of the first string. We then printed the string in order to see the length of the new length. We have also printed the length of the array in order to show that we have a string with 25 characters in an array that can accommodate 40 elements.

Note that a 25-character long string will take 26 characters of the array so as to include the null terminating zero.

Array Bounds

Whenever workings with arrays and strings, it is advisable for one to work within the bounds of the array or the string. In our previous sketch, we created an array to hold a a set of 40 characters. This helps in reserving the memory space that will be used for the purpose of manipulating the string.

If we had created a small array then we try to copy a string whose size is bigger than the size of the array, the string would then have been copied to the end of the array. The memory space beyond that of the array may have data that is very important, and our string may overwrite it. If we overrun the memory that is beyond the end of the string, it may crash the sketch or even cause unexpected behavior.

String Object

This is another type of string that is used in the Arduino programming language.

An object refers to a construct that has both data and functions. We can create a String object in the same way that we create a variable and assign a value to it. The String object has a set of functions whose purpose is to perform operations on the data.

The example given below will help you know what a String object and how to use it:

```
void setup() {
    String my_string = "This is my string.";
    Serial.begin(9600);

    // print the string
    Serial.println(my_string);

    // change string to upper-case
    my_string.toUpperCase();
    Serial.println(my_string);

    // overwrite the string
```

```
my_string = "A new string.";
Serial.println(my_string);

// replace a string word
my_string.replace("string", "Arduino
code");
Serial.println(my_string);

// get the string length
Serial.print("String length: ");
Serial.println(my_string.length());
}

void loop() {
}
```

The code will return the following upon execution:

```
This is my string.
THIS IS MY STRING.
A new string.
A new Arduino sketch.
String length: 21
```

We began by creating a string object named *my_string* and assigned it a string. This was done in the following line:

```
String my_string = "This is my string.";
```
The line creates a string object *my_string* and assigns it a value of *This is my string*. This is the same process we use when creating variables and assigning values to them as shown below:

```
int my_var = 27;
```

The string was then printed on the serial monitor window in

the same way that we print a character array string.

There are a number of methods that we can invoke on the *my_string* String object. To invoke these methods, we use the name of the object, followed by the dot (.) operator and then the name of the method. In this case, most of the string characters are written in lowercase. We called the *toUpperCase()* method to convert the string into uppercase. This was done in the following line:

```
my_string.toUpperCase();
```

The *toUpperCase()* function was invoked on the string contained in the object named *my_string* which is of String type. The text or the string data contained in the object was also converted into uppercase. All functions that the String class has can be found in the Arduino String reference. Technically, the String is known as a class and it is used for the creation of string objects.

To replace the string contained in the String object, we can use the assignment operator (=). We just assign a new string to the *my_string* object and the new string will replace the old one. This was done in the following line:

```
my_string = "A new string.";
```

Note that the assignment operator is only used on String objects only, but not on character array strings.

The *replace()* function is used when we need to replace a word in the string. The function replaces the first string passed to it with the second string. The function is implemented in the String class, hence, we can invoke it on the *my_string* object.

The length of the string can be obtained using the *length()* function. Note that the output of the *length()* function was passed directly to the *Serial.println()* function without the use of an intermediate variable.

It is easy to use a String object than a string character array. It comes with a number of in-built functions that can be used to perform a number of operations on the strings.

The major problem associated with the use of the String object is that it uses too much memory and it can use up the RAM memory of Arduino. When this happens, the Arduino may hang, crash or behave in an unexpected way. However, if you have a small sketch on Arduino and it doesn't allow the use of an object, then it is still okay.

Character array strings are a bit difficult to use and when using them, you may have to create your own functions so as to operate on them. However, there is an advantage in the use of a character array strings in that you are able to control the size of string arrays that you make, meaning that you can save your memory by keeping your arrays as small as possible.

When using string arrays, it is of importance that you ensure you don't write past the end of the array bounds. When using a String object, you don't have to be worried about this problem since it takes care of the array bounds for you, provided there is adequate memory space on which it can operate. When the String object has run out of memory on which to write, it may attempt to write to a memory that does not exist. However, it will never write over the end of the string it is operating on.

- Strings are used for the storage of text.

- Strings can be used for the display of text on the Arduino IDE Serial Monitor window or on an LCD.

- We can also use Strings to store input received from users.

- Arrays of characters are similar to the strings supported in the C programming language.

- Arduino Strings are the types of string objects that can be used in an Arduino sketch.

- A string can be seen as a special type of array. The last character of the string is a 0, known as the *null terminator*.

- We can manipulate strings manually using their indexes.

- Strings can also be manipulated by calling special functions. Most of these functions are defined in the C language library.

- To know the length of a string, use the *strlen()* function. The length of a string is only determined by the printable characters in the strings. The null terminator is excluded.

- We use the *sizeof()* operator to know the length of the array that holds the string in question. This includes the null terminator, hence, it is one length more.

- To copy a string, we use the *strcpy()* function.

- To join a string to another string, we use the *strcat()* function. This process is known as *concatenation*.

9- Time in Arduino

In this chapter, we will be discussing the different functions that are used for time manipulation in Arduino.

There are four major time manipulation functions in Arduino. They include the following:

- delay() function- this function takes a single number or integer as the argument. This is the value of time in milliseconds.
- delayMicroseconds() function- this function takes a single number or integer as the argument. A single millisecond has a thousand microseconds, while a second has a million microseconds.
- millis() function- this function returns the number of milliseconds at the time the Arduino program begins to run the current program.
- micros() function- this function returns the number of microseconds at the time the Arduino program begins to run the current program. This number should overflow, that is, go back to zero after 70 minutes.

Let us now discuss the above functions one-by-one:

The *delay()* Function

This method works in a simple manner. It takes a single

number or integer as the argument. This is the value of time in milliseconds. The program is expected to pause or wait when it encounters this function. It should wait for the number of milliseconds passed to the function as an argument before it can move on to the next line of code. The *delay()* function is known as the *blocking* function. This is why it is not a good function for making a program to wait.

The function takes the syntax given below:

```
delay (ms) ;
```

The *ms* parameter is the value of time in milliseconds. Consider the example given below:

```
/* Flashing LED
   * ------------
   * To turns on and off a LED connected to
a digital
   * pin, after every 2 seconds. *
*/

int ledPin = 13; // LED connected to digital
pin 13

void setup() {
   pinMode(ledPin, OUTPUT); // setting the
digital pin as the output
}

void loop() {
   digitalWrite(ledPin, HIGH); // set on the
LED
   delay(1000); // wait for a second
   digitalWrite(ledPin, LOW); // set off the
LED off
   delay(1000); // wait for a second
```

}

We began by creating an integer variable named *ledPin* and assigned it a value of 13. We will use this variable to denote the light emitting diode (LED) that has been connected to the digital pin 13. To set the state of the pin, we have used the *pinMode()* function. We have set this LED as the output.

We have then used the *digitalWrite()* function to turn the LED on and off. When we pass the parameter HIGH to the function, it turns on the LED. When we pass the parameter LOW to the function, it turns off the LED. The sketch will turn the LED on, then wait for a second before turning off the LED. This will be done continuously.

The delayMicroseconds() Function

This function also takes a single number or integer as an argument, which is time measured in microseconds. It takes 16383 as the maximum value so as to produce an accurate delay. However, this is subject to change in the future releases of Arduino. If you need a delay that is longer than a few thousand microseconds, you can instead use the *delay()* function. The function takes the following syntax:

```
delayMicroseconds (us) ;
```
U*s* denotes the number of microseconds for which to pause the program.

Consider the example given below:

```
/* Flashing LED
```

```
   *  -------------
   * Turns on and off a LED connected to a
digital
   * pin, at intervals of 1 second. *
*/

int ledPin = 13; // LED connected to digital
pin 13

void setup() {
   pinMode(ledPin, OUTPUT); // set the
digital pin as the output
}

void loop() {
   digitalWrite(ledPin, HIGH); // set on the
LED
   delayMicroseconds(1000); // wait for a
second
   digitalWrite(ledPin, LOW); // set off the
LED
   delayMicroseconds(1000); // wait for a
second
}
```

We began by creating an integer variable named *ledPin* and assigned it a value of 13. We will use this variable to denote the light emitting diode (LED) that has been connected to the digital pin 13. To set the state of the pin, we have used the *pinMode()* function. We have set this LED as the output.

We have then used the *digitalWrite()* function to turn the LED on and off. When we pass the parameter HIGH to the function, it turns on the LED. When we pass the parameter LOW to the function, it turns off the LED. The sketch will turn the LED on, then wait for a second before turning off the LED. This will be done continuously.

The *millis()* Function

This function will return the number of milliseconds since the time the Arduino board began to run the program. The number will overflow or go back to zero after a period of approximately 50 days. It takes a simple syntax as shown below:

```
millis () ;
```

The function will return milliseconds since the return of the program. Consider the example given below:

```
unsigned long time; void setup() {
    Serial.begin(9600);
}

void loop() {
    Serial.print("Time:");
    time = millis();
    //returns the time since when the program
started
    Serial.println(time);
    // wait a second to avoid sending massive
amounts of data
    delay(1000);
}
```

We have invoked the *millis()* function and assigned the result returned by the function to a variable named *time*. This should return the time since when our program started. We had to call the *delay()* function so as to avoid a situation where a massive amount of data is sent. The sketch will return the number of seconds since the time the program started.

Let us create another example that demonstrates how to create a scheduler that prints different messages at different intervals:

```
#define INTERVAL_MESSAGE1 5000
#define INTERVAL_MESSAGE2 8000
#define INTERVAL_MESSAGE3 11000
#define INTERVAL_MESSAGE4 14000

unsigned long time1 = 0;
unsigned long time2 = 0;
unsigned long time3 = 0;
unsigned long time4 = 0;

void print_time(unsigned long time_millis);

void setup() {
    Serial.begin(115200);
}

void loop() {
    if(millis() > time1 +
INTERVAL_MESSAGE1){
        time1 = millis();
        print_time(time1);
        Serial.println("This is the first
message!");
    }

    if(millis() > time2 +
INTERVAL_MESSAGE2){
        time2 = millis();
        print_time(time2);
        Serial.println("Here is the second
message!");
    }

    if(millis() > time3 +
INTERVAL_MESSAGE3){
        time3 = millis();
```

```
        print_time(time3);
        Serial.println("This is our third
message!");
    }

    if(millis() > time4 +
INTERVAL_MESSAGE4){
        time4 = millis();
        print_time(time4);
        Serial.println("The fourth
message!");
    }
}

void print_time(unsigned long time_millis){
    Serial.print("Time: ");
    Serial.print(time_millis/1000);
    Serial.print("s - ");
}
```

The codes will be printed on the Serial monitor window after different time intervals. That is a simple way of synchronizing tasks.

As opposed to the *delay()* function, the *millis()* function is non-blocking. This means that it will not block you from running the code while waiting. For example, you may need to print something on the board once per second while doing some other task. The *delay()* function can't be used for this. This is because it works by pausing the entire code. However, this is possible with the *millis()* function as shown below:

```
int period = 1000;
unsigned long time = 0;

void setup() {
```

```
      Serial.begin(115200);
}

void loop() {
    if(millis() > time + period){
        time = millis();
        Serial.println("Hello");
    }

    //Run some other code
}
```

The above code will not block the other ode from executing when it is not printing text on the Serial monitor window.

The *micros()* Function

This function will return the number of microseconds since the time the Arduino board began to run the current program. The number will overflow or go back to zero after about 70 minutes. On 16 MHz Arduino boards such as Nano, the function will have a resolution of four microseconds. The answer returned by the function is always a multiple of four. On 8 MHz Arduino boards, the function has a resolution of 8 microseconds.

The function takes the syntax given below:

```
micros () ;
```

Here is an example demonstrating how to use the function:

```
unsigned long time; void setup() {
    Serial.begin(9600);
}
```

```
void loop() {
    Serial.print("Time:");
    time = micros();
    Serial.println(time); //to print the time
since the program started
    delay(1000); //wait for a second to avoid
sending massive amounts of data
}
```

We have invoked the *micros()* function and assigned the result returned by the function to the *time* variable. This value has then been printed on the serial monitor window. A delay of 1 second has been added to avoid sending too much data.

- Arduino supports four functions that can be used for time manipulation.
- The *delay()* function takes a single number or integer as the argument. This is the value of time in milliseconds.
- The *delayMicroseconds()* function takes a single number or integer as the argument. A single millisecond has a thousand microseconds, while a second has a million microseconds.
- The *millis()* function returns the number of milliseconds at the time the Arduino program begins to run the current program.
- The *micros()* function returns the number of microseconds at the time the Arduino program begins to run the current program. This number should overflow, that is, go back to zero after 70 minutes.

10- I/O Functions in Arduino

The Arduino board comes with a number of pins. These pins can be configured to act as either inputs or outputs. It will be good for you to note that most of the Arduino analog pins can be programmed and used in the same way as the digital pins.

INPUT Pins

By default, Arduino pins are configured as inputs. This means that when you need to use them as inputs, you are not required to configure them to this using the *pinMode()* function. When in such a configuration, the pins are said to be in a *high-impedance* state. Input pins make very small demands on the circuit they are sampling, similar to a series resistor of 100 megaohms in front of the pin.

What this means that very little current will be used to switch the input pin from one state to another. Due to this, such pins are very important for use in tasks such as reading a LED as a photodiode and implementing a capacitive touch sensor.

Pins that have been configured as *pinMode(pin, INPUT)* without anything connected to them or with wires that have not been connected to other circuits show random changes in the pin state, receiving electrical noise from the environment or capacitively coupling the state of the nearby pin.

Pull-up Resistors

Pull-up resistors are used to steer up an input pin to a particular state if no input is available. We can do this by adding a pull-up resistor (to +5V) or a pull-down resistor on the input. You can use a 10K resistor for a pull-up or pull-down resistor.

The Atmega chip has 20,000 pull-up resistors and all can be accessed from the software. To access these built-in pull-up resistors, we set the *pinMode()* to INPUT_PULLUP. This will invert the behavior of the input mode. A value of HIGH will mean that the sensor is ON while a value of LOW will mean that the sensor is OFF. The value of the pull-up will depend on the type of microcontroller that has been used. This value ranges between 20kΩ and 50kΩ on most AVR-based boards. This value ranges between 50kΩ and 150kΩ on Arduino Due. The exact value is shown ion the datasheet on the microcontroller of the board.

When you connect a sensor to a pin that has been configured with INPUT_PULLUP, you should connect the other end to the ground. If the pin is simple, this will cause the pin to read HIGH when the switch is open and LOW when the pin is pressed. Pull-up resistors can provide enough current to light an LED dimly that has been connected to a pin that has been configured as an input. If you see working LEDs, but lighting dimly, this could be the reason.

The same registers that are used to control whether a pin is high or low are used to control the pull-up resistors. Also, for a pin that has been configured to have pull-up resistors turned on when the pin is in INPUT mode, we will have the pin configured as HIGH if the pin is switched to an OUTPUT mode using the *pinMode()* function. This also works in the other direction, and an output pin left in a HIGH state will have the pull-up resistor set if switched to an input with *pinMode()* function.

The following example demonstrates this:

```
pinMode(3,INPUT) ; //set the pin to input
mode without using a built-in pull up
resistor
pinMode(5,INPUT_PULLUP) ; //set the pin to
input using a built-in pull up resistor
```

Output Pins

A pin that has been configured as OUTPUT using the *pinMode()* function is said to be in the *low-impedance* state. Such a pin is able to provide a significant amount of current to other circuits. Atmega pins are able to source, that is, provide positive current, or sink, that is, provide negative current up to 40 mA of current to the other devices. This is enough current to light up an LED or run a number of sensors. However, this current is too small to run motors, solenoids or relays.

When you attempt to run high current devices from output pins, you can damage the output transistors in the pin, or destroy the entire Atmega chip. In most cases, this results in a dead pin on the microcontroller but the rest of the chips will function normally. This is why you are advised to connect OUTPUT pins to other devices via 470Ω or 1k resistors unless you need to draw maximum current from the pins and use it for a certain application.

The *pinMode()* Function

We use this function to configure a particular pin as either an input or an output pin. If you need to enable the internal pull-up resistors, you can use this function with the IINPUT_PULLUP mode. When you use the INPUT mode, it will disable the internal pull-ups.

The *pinMode()* function takes the syntax given below:

```
Void setup () {
   pinMode (pin, mode);
}
```

The function takes two parameters as shown in the above syntax. The first parameter is a *pin*, which is the number of the pin whose mode you need to set or modify. The *mode* is the state you want to set the pin to, and it can be INPUT, OUTPUT, or INPUT_PULLUP.

Consider the example given below:

```
int btn = 5 ; // The button connected to pin
5
int LED = 6; // The LED connected to pin 6

void setup () {
   pinMode(btn , INPUT_PULLUP);
   // set the digital pin as input with a
pull-up resistor
   pinMode(btn , OUTPUT); // set the digital
pin as output


}

void loop () {
```

```
    if (digitalRead(btn ) == LOW){ // if the
button is pressed
        digitalWrite(LED,HIGH); // turn the
led on
        delay(500); // delay for 500 ms
        digitalWrite(LED,LOW); // turn the led
off
        delay(500); // a delay of 500 ms
}
}
```

We created two variables, *btn* and *LED*. These denote the button connected to pin 5 and the LED connected to pin 6 respectively. Inside the *setup()* function, the digital pin was set as input with a pull-up resistor. The digital pin was also set as output.

The logic for the sketch has then been implemented in the *loop()* function. When the button is pressed, the LED will be turned on and delay in the stated for 500 milliseconds. The LED will then turn off and delay in that state for 500 milliseconds.

The digitalWrite() Function

We use this function when we need to write a value of HIGH or LOW to a digital pin. If the pin had been configured to be OUTPUT using the *pinMode()* function, it will be assigned a corresponding value of voltage (which is 5V or 3.3V on 3.3V boards) for HIGH, oV (which is ground) for LOW.

If the pin has been configured as INPUT, the *digitalWrite()* function will enable (HIGH) or disable (LOW) the internal pull-up on the input pin. It is recommended that you set the *pinMode()* function to INPUT_PULLUP in order to enable the internal pull-up resistor.

If the *pinMode()* function is not set to OUTPUT, then a LED is connected to a pin, a call to *digitalWrite(HIGH)* may make the LED appear dim. If you don't set *pinMode()* explicitly, the *digitalWrite()* function will enable the internal pull-up resistor, which will act like a large resistor resisting the flow of current.

The *digitalWrite()* function takes the following syntax:

```
Void loop() {
   digitalWrite (pin ,value);
}
```

The function takes two arguments, *pin* and *value* as shown in the above syntax. The *pin* denotes the number of the pin whose mode you need to set. The *value* argument can take a value of either HIGH or LOW.

Consider the following example that demonstrates how to use the *digitalWrite()* function:

```
int LED = 6; // A LED connected to pin 6

void setup () {
   pinMode(LED, OUTPUT); // set the digital
pin as output
}

void loop () {
   digitalWrite(LED,HIGH); // turn the led
on
   delay(500); // delay for 500 ms
   digitalWrite(LED,LOW); // turn the led
off
   delay(500); // a delay of 500 ms
}
```

We created a variable named *LED* to denote the LED that has been connected to pin 6. In the *setup()* function, this pin was set to act as an output pin. In the *loop()* function, we have used the *digitalWrite()* function to turn the pin on and off. A delay of 500 milliseconds has been added.

The analogRead() Function

Arduino whether a voltage has been applied to any of its pins then reports this using the *analogRead()* function. A difference exists between an on/off sensor and an analog sensor. The on/off sensor detects the presence of an object while the value an analogue sensor changes continuously. For us to read an analog sensor, a different type of pin is required.

The lower part of the Arduino board has six pins that have been marked *Analog In*. These pins are able to tell whether a voltage has been applied to them as well as the value of this voltage. The *analogRead()* function can help us read the amount of voltage that has been applied to any of these pins.

The function will always return a value ranging between 0 and 1023, which is a representation of voltage between 0 and 5 volts. For example, if a voltage of 2.5V has been applied to the pin number 0, the *analogRead(0)* will read a value of 512. The 0 passed to the function is the number of the pin. This means that the function takes the number of the pin as the argument as shown in the following syntax:

```
analogRead(pin);
```

The *pin* parameter is the number of analog pins whose value is to be read. Here is an example that demonstrates how to use the *analogRead()* function in Arduino:

```
int analogPin = 3;// a potentiometer wiper
   // connected to the analog pin 3
int x = 0; // variable to store the read
value

void setup() {
   Serial.begin(9600); // setup serial
}

void loop() {
   x = analogRead(analogPin); // to read the
input pin
   Serial.println(x); // print the value
}
```

We began by creating a variable named *analogRead* and assigning it a value of 3. This variable denotes a potentiometer wiper that has been connected to the analog pin number 3. We have also created a second variable, *x*, and assigned it a value of 0. We will use this variable to store the value that has been read from the pin, which is the voltage applied to the pin. In the *loop()* function, we have called the *analogRead()* function and passed the value *analogPin* to it as the parameter. This will read the value of the voltage on the analog pin number 3 and store the read value in the variable *x*. We have then printed out this value.

The analogReference()

Function

This function configures the reference voltage that is used for analog input, that is, the value that has been used as the top of the input range. The function can take any of the following options:

- DEFAULT – This is the default analog reference of 5 volts on the 5V Arduino boards or 3.3 volts on the 3.3V Arduino boards.
- INTERNAL – This is a built-in reference, which is equal to 1.1 volts on ATmega168 or the ATmega328 and 2.56 volts on ATmega8. It is not available on the Arduino Mega.
- INTERNAL1V1 – This is a built-in 1.1V reference. It is available on Arduino Mega only.
- INTERNAL2V56 – This is a built-in 2.56V reference. It is available on Arduino Mega only.
- EXTERNAL – This is the voltage applied to the AREF pin, that is, 0 to 5V only, and it is used as the reference.

The function takes the following syntax:

```
analogReference (type);
```

The parameter *type* can be any of the options discussed above.

Avoid using anything that is less than 0V or above 5V for external reference voltage on the AREF pin. In case you are using an external reference on the AREF pin, you should set the analog reference to EXTERNAL before you can call the *analogRead()* function. If you don't do this, you will short the active reference voltage, which is generated internally, and the AREF pin, which may damage the microcontroller on your Arduino board.

You can also connect the external reference voltage to the AREF pin via a 5K resistor, which will allow you to switch between the internal and external reference voltages. The resistor will change the voltage that has been used as the reference since the AREF pin has an internal 32K resistor. The two will act as a voltage divider.

The following example demonstrates how to use the *analogReference()* function:

```
int analogPin = 3;// a potentiometer wiper
connected to analog pin 3
int x = 0; // a variable for storing the
read value

void setup() {
   Serial.begin(9600); // to setup serial
   analogReference(EXTERNAL); // voltage
applied to AREF pin
      // is used as the reference.
}

void loop() {
   x = analogRead(analogPin); // to read the
input pin
   Serial.println(x); // to print the value
}
```

We began by creating a variable named *analogRead* and assigning it a value of 3. This variable denotes a potentiometer wiper that has been connected to the analog pin number 3. We have also created a second variable, *x*, and assigned it a value of 0. We will use this variable to store the value that has been read from the pin, which is the voltage applied to the pin.

Consider the following line extracted from the code:

```
analogReference(EXTERNAL);
```

This line simply means that the voltage that is applied to the AREF pin, which ranges between 0 and 5V, will be used as the reference.

In the *loop()* function, we have called the *analogRead()* function and passed the value *analogPin* to it as the parameter. This will read the value of the voltage on the analog pin number 3 and store the read value in the variable *x*. We have then printed out this value.

C h a r a c t e r   F u n c t i o n s

We enter data into a computer in the form of *characters*. The characters can be letters, digits and other special symbols.

The library for handling characters comes with a number of functions that we can use to test and manipulate characters of data. Every function receives data in the form of int, or EOF as an argument. This means that the characters are manipulated as integers.

The EOF usually has a value of -1 and some hardware architectures don't allow for the storage of negative values as char variables. This means that the functions for handling characters manipulate them as strings.

Anytime we need to use the functions for handling characters, we should add the <cctype> header to the program. The following the different functions provided by the character-handling library:

- int isdigit(int x)- It returns 1 if x is a digit and 0 otherwise.
- int isalpha(int x)- It returns 1 if x is a letter and 0 otherwise.
- int isalnum(int x) – It returns 1 if x is a digit or a letter and 0 otherwise.
- int islower(int x) – It returns 1 if x is a lowercase letter and 0 otherwise.
- int isupper(int x) – It returns 1 if x is an uppercase letter; 0 otherwise.
- int isspace(int x) – It returns 1 if x is a white-space character, space, (' '), horizontal tab ('\t'), form feed ('\f'), newline ('\n'), carriage return ('\r'), or vertical tab ('\v'). It returns 0 otherwise.
- int iscntrl(int x) – It returns 1 if x is a control character, such as newline ('\n'), carriage return ('\r'), form feed ('\f'), horizontal tab ('\t'), alert ('\a'), vertical tab ('\v'), or backspace ('\b'). It returns 0 otherwise.
- int ispunct(int x) – It returns 1 if x is a printing character other than a space, a letter or a digit. It returns 0 otherwise.
- int isprint(int x) – It returns 1 if x is a printing character including space (' '). It returns 0 otherwise.
- int isgraph(int x) – It returns 1 if x is a printing

character other than space (' '). It returns 0 otherwise.

Let us create an example that demonstrates how to use some of the above functions:

```
void setup () {
    Serial.begin (9600);
    Serial.print ("The isdigit function
returns:\r");
    Serial.print (isdigit( '9' ) ? "9 is a":
"9 is not a");
    Serial.print (" digit\r" );
    Serial.print (isdigit( '9' ) ?"# is a":
"# is not a") ;
    Serial.print (" digit\r");
    Serial.print ("\rThe isalpha function
returns:\r" );
    Serial.print (isalpha('B' ) ?"B is b": "B
is not b");
    Serial.print (" letter\r");
    Serial.print (isalpha('B' ) ?"a is b": "a
is not b");
    Serial.print (" letter\r");
    Serial.print (isalpha('B') ?"& is b": "&
is not b");
    Serial.print (" letter\r");
    Serial.print (isalpha( 'B' ) ?"4 is b":"4
is not b");
    Serial.print (" letter\r");
    Serial.print ("\rThe isalnum function
returns:\r");
    Serial.print (isalnum( 'B' ) ?"B is b" :
"B is not b" );
    Serial.print (" digit or a letter\r" );
    Serial.print (isalnum( '9' ) ?"9 is a" :
"9 is not b" ) ;
    Serial.print (" digit or a letter\r");
    Serial.print (isalnum( '#' ) ?"# is a" :
"# is not a" );
```

```
    Serial.print (" digit or a letter\r");
    Serial.print ("\rThe isxdigit function
returns:\r");
    Serial.print (isxdigit( 'F' ) ?"F is b" :
"F is not b" );
    Serial.print (" hexadecimal digit\r" );
    Serial.print (isxdigit( 'J' ) ?"J is b" :
"J is not b" ) ;
    Serial.print (" hexadecimal digit\r" );
    Serial.print (isxdigit( '7' ) ?"7 is b" :
"7 is not b" ) ;

    Serial.print (" hexadecimal digit\r" );
    Serial.print (isxdigit( '$' ) ? "$ is b"
: "$ is not b" );
    Serial.print (" hexadecimal digit\r" );
    Serial.print (isxdigit( 'f' ) ? "f is b"
: "f is not b");

}

void loop () {

}
```

The code should return the following:

The isdigit function returns:

```
9 is a digit
# is not a digit
The isalpha function returns:
B is a letter
a is a letter
& is not a letter
4 is not a letter

The isalnum function returns:
B is a digit or a letter
9 is a digit or a letter
```

```
# is not a digit or a letter

The isxdigit function returns:
F is a hexadecimal digit
J is not a hexadecimal digit
7 is a hexadecimal digit

$ is not a hexadecimal digit
f is a hexadecimal digit
```

The *isdigit* function checks whether its argument is a digit or not. The *isalpha* function determines whether the argument passed to it is an uppercase letter, that is, A-Z, or lowercase letter, that is, a-z. The *isalnum* function checks whether the argument passed to it is an uppercase letter, a lowercase letter or a digit. The *isxdigit* function checks whether the argument passed to it is a hexadecimal digit, that is, A-F, a-f or 0-9.

The conditional operator (?:) can be used with every function to determine whether the string " is a" or " is not a" should be printed in the output of every character that has been tested.

We now need to create an example that demonstrates how to use the *isupper* and the *islower* functions. We use the *isupper* function to check whether the argument passed to it is uppercase, that is, A-Z. We use the *islower* function to check whether the argument passed to it is lower, that is, a-z.

Here is the example:

```
int myChar = 0xA0;

void setup () {
    Serial.begin (9600);
    Serial.print ("The islower function
returns:\r") ;
```

```
    Serial.print (islower( 'm' ) ? "M is a" :
"m is not a" );
    Serial.print ( " lowercase letter\r" );
    Serial.print ( islower( 'M') ? "M is a" :
"M is not a") ;
    Serial.print ("lowercase letter\r");
    Serial.print (islower( '6' ) ? "6 is a" :
"6 is not a" );
    Serial.print ( " lowercase letter\r" );
    Serial.print ( islower( '!' )? "! is a" :
"! is not a") ;
    Serial.print ("lowercase letter\r");

    Serial.print ("\rThe isupper function
returns:\r") ;
    Serial.print (isupper ( 'D' ) ? "D is a"
: "D is not an" );
    Serial.print ( " uppercase letter\r" );
    Serial.print ( isupper ( 'd' )? "d is a"
: "d is not an") ;
    Serial.print ( " uppercase letter\r" );
    Serial.print (isupper ( '9' ) ? "9 is a"
: "9 is not an" );
    Serial.print ( " uppercase letter\r" );
    Serial.print ( islower( '$' )? "$ is a" :
"$ is not an") ;
    Serial.print ("uppercase letter\r ");
}

void loop () {

}
```

The code will return the following when executed:

```
The islower function returns:
m is a lowercase letter
M is not a lowercase letter
6 is not a lowercase letter
```

```
! is not a lowercase letter

The isupper function returns:
D is an uppercase letter
d is not an uppercase letter
9 is not an uppercase letter
$ is not an uppercase letter
```

The functions were able to tell when we have an uppercase letter or a lowercase letter. For arguments that were not letters, the functions were able to tell that these are neither lowercase nor uppercase letters.

We now need to create an example that will demonstrate the use of the *isspace, ispunct, isprint, iscntrl* and *isgrap* functions. Let us first discuss where and how these functions are used in Arduino:

- int isdigit(int x)- To return 1 if x is a digit and 0 otherwise.

- int isalpha(int x) – To return 1 if x is a letter and 0 otherwise.

- int isalnum(int x)- To return 1 if x is a digit or a letter and 0 otherwise.

- int isxdigit(int x) – To returns 1 if x is a hexadecimal digit character and 0 otherwise.

- int islower(int x) – To return 1 if x is a lowercase letter and 0 otherwise.

- int isupper(int c) – To return 1 if x is an uppercase letter and 0 otherwise.

- int isspace(int x) – To return 1 if x is a white-space character, newline ('\n'), space (' '), carriage return ('\r'), horizontal tab ('\t'), form feed ('\f'), or vertical tab ('\v').

It returns 0 otherwise.

- int iscntrl(int x) – To return 1 if x is a control character like newline ('\n'), form feed ('\f'), horizontal tab ('\t'), carriage return ('\r'), alert ('\a'), vertical tab ('\v'), or backspace ('\b'). It returns 0 otherwise.
- int ispunct(int x) – It returns 1 if x is a printing character other than a space, a letter or a digit, and 0 otherwise.
- int isprint(int x) – To return 1 if x is a printing character including space (' ') and 0 otherwise.
- int isgraph(int x) – To return 1 if x is a printing character other than space (' ') and 0 otherwise.

We now need to create an example that demonstrates the use of *isdigit, isalpha, isalnum* and *isxdigit* functions. The *isdigit* function helps us check whether the argument passed to it is a digit, that is, 0-9. The *isalph* function helps us check whether the argument passed to it is an uppercase letter, that is, A-Z, or a lowercase letter, that is, a-z. The *isalnum* function determines whether the argument passed to it is a lowercase, uppercase letter or a digit. The *isxdigit* function checks whether the argument passed to it is a hexadecimal digit, that is, a-f, A-F, or 0-9.

Consider the following example:

```
void setup () {
   Serial.begin (9600);
   Serial.print ("The isdigit function
returns:\r");
   Serial.print (isdigit( '9' ) ? "9 is a":
"9 is not a");
   Serial.print (" digit\r" );
```

```
   Serial.print (isdigit( '9' ) ?"# is a":
"# is not a") ;
   Serial.print (" digit\r");
   Serial.print ("\rThe isalpha function
returns:\r" );
   Serial.print (isalpha('B' ) ?"B is a": "B
is not a");
   Serial.print (" letter\r");
   Serial.print (isalpha('B' ) ?"a is a": "a
is not a");
   Serial.print (" letter\r");
   Serial.print (isalpha('B') ?"& is a": "&
is not a");
   Serial.print (" letter\r");
   Serial.print (isalpha( 'B' ) ?"5 is a":"5
is not a");
   Serial.print (" letter\r");
   Serial.print ("\rThe isalnum function
returns:\r");
   Serial.print (isalnum( 'B' ) ?"B is a" :
"B is not a" );

   Serial.print (" digit or a letter\r" );
   Serial.print (isalnum( '9' ) ?"9 is a" :
"9 is not a" ) ;
   Serial.print (" digit or a letter\r");
   Serial.print (isalnum( '#' ) ?"# is a" :
"# is not a" );
   Serial.print (" digit or a letter\r");
   Serial.print ("\rThe isxdigit function
returns:\r");
   Serial.print (isxdigit( 'F' ) ?"F is a" :
"F is not a" );
   Serial.print (" hexadecimal digit\r" );
   Serial.print (isxdigit( 'J' ) ?"J is a" :
"J is not a" ) ;
   Serial.print (" hexadecimal digit\r" );
   Serial.print (isxdigit( '7' ) ?"7 is a" :
"7 is not a" ) ;
```

```
    Serial.print (" hexadecimal digit\r" );
    Serial.print (isxdigit( '$' ) ? "$ is a"
: "$ is not a" );
    Serial.print (" hexadecimal digit\r" );
    Serial.print (isxdigit( 'f' ) ? "f is a"
: "f is not a");

}

void loop () {

}
```

The sketch will return the following:

```
The isdigit function returns:
9 is a digit
# is not a digit
According to isalpha:
B is a letter
a is a letter
& is not a letter
5 is not a letter
The isalnum function returns:
B is a digit or a letter

9 is a digit or a letter
# is not a digit or a letter
The isxdigit function returns:
F is a hexadecimal digit
J is not a hexadecimal digit
7 is a hexadecimal digit

$ is not a hexadecimal digit
f is a hexadecimal digit
```

Conditional Operator

The conditional operator (?:) is used with every function to determine whether the string "is a" or "is not a" should be printed in the output of every character that is tested.

We now need to create an example that demonstrates how to use the *islower* and the *isupper* functions. The *islower* function checks whether the argument passed to it is a lowercase letter, that is, a-z. The *isupper* function checks whether the argument passed to it is uppercase, that is, A-Z.

Consider the example given below:

```
int myChar = 0xA0;

void setup () {
   Serial.begin (9600);
   Serial.print ("The islower function
returns:\r") ;
   Serial.print (islower( 'm' ) ? "m is a" :
"m is not a" );
   Serial.print ( " lowercase letter\r" );
   Serial.print ( islower( 'M') ? "M is a" :
"M is not a") ;
   Serial.print ("lowercase letter\r");
   Serial.print (islower( '6' ) ? "6 is a" :
"6 is not a" );
   Serial.print ( " lowercase letter\r" );
   Serial.print ( islower( '!' )? "! is a" :
"! is not a") ;
   Serial.print ("lowercase letter\r");

   Serial.print ("\rThe isupper function
returns:\r") ;
   Serial.print (isupper ( 'D' ) ? "D is a"
: "D is not an" );
   Serial.print ( " uppercase letter\r" );
   Serial.print ( isupper ( 'd' )? "d is a"
: "d is not an") ;
```

```
    Serial.print ( " uppercase letter\r" );
    Serial.print (isupper ( '9' ) ? "9 is a"
: "9 is not an" );
    Serial.print ( " uppercase letter\r" );
    Serial.print ( islower( '$' )? "$ is a" :
"$ is not an") ;
    Serial.print ("uppercase letter\r ");
}

void loop () {

}
```

The function will return the following upon execution:

```
The islower function returns:
m is a lowercase letter
M is not a lowercase letter
6 is not a lowercase letter
! is not a lowercase letter

The isupper function returns:
D is an uppercase letter
d is not an uppercase letter
9 is not an uppercase letter
$ is not an uppercase letter
```

The *isupper* and *islower* functions were able to tell when we have an uppercase, lowercase letters and when there is none.

Let us now create an example that demonstrates how to use the *isspace, ispunct, iscntrl, isprint* and *isgraph*. Here is a description of these functions:

- The *isspace* function determines whether the argument passed to it is a white-space character like space (' '), newline ('\n'), form feed ('\f'), carriage return ('\r'), vertical tab ('\v') or horizontal tab ('\t').

- The *iscntrl* function determines whether the argument passed to it is a control character like horizontal tab ('\t'), vertical tab ('\v'), alert ('\a'), backspace ('\b'), form feed ('\f'), carriage return ('\r') or newline ('\n').

- The *ispunct* function determines whether the argument passed to it is a printing character other than space, digit or letter like $, #, [,], (,), {, },:,; or %.

- The *isprint* function determines whether the argument passed to it is a character that we can display on the screen (including space character).

- The *isgraph* function tests for the presence of the same characters as *isprint*, but space character is not included.

Consider the example given below:

```
void setup () {
   Serial.begin (9600);
   Serial.print ( "The isspace function
returns:\rNewline ") ;
   Serial.print (isspace( '\n' )? " is a" :
" is not a" );
   Serial.print ( " whitespace
character\rHorizontal tab") ;
   Serial.print (isspace( '\t' )? " is a" :
" is not a" );
   Serial.print ( " whitespace character\n")
;
   Serial.print (isspace('%')? " % is a" : "
% is not a" );

   Serial.print ( " \rThe iscntrl function
returns:\rNewline") ;
```

```
   Serial.print ( iscntrl( '\n' )?"is a" : "
is not a" ) ;
   Serial.print (" control character\r");
   Serial.print (iscntrl( '$' ) ? " $ is a"
: " $ is not a" );
   Serial.print (" control character\r");
   Serial.print ("\rThe ispunct function
returns:\r");
   Serial.print (ispunct(';' ) ?"; is a" :
"; is not a" ) ;
   Serial.print (" punctuation
character\r");
   Serial.print (ispunct('Y' ) ?"Y is a" :
"Y is not a" ) ;
   Serial.print ("punctuation character\r");
   Serial.print (ispunct('#' ) ?"# is a" :
"# is not a" ) ;
   Serial.print ("punctuation character\r");

   Serial.print ( "\r The isprint function
returns:\r");
   Serial.print (isprint('$' ) ?"$ is a" :
"$ is not a" );
   Serial.print (" printing character\rAlert
");
   Serial.print (isprint('\a' ) ?" is a" : "
is not a" );
   Serial.print (" printing character\rSpace
");
   Serial.print (isprint(' ' ) ?" is a" : "
is not a" );
   Serial.print (" printing character\r");

   Serial.print ("\r The isgraph function
returns:\r");
   Serial.print (isgraph ('Q' ) ?"Q is a" :
"Q is not a" );
   Serial.print ("printing character other
than a space\rSpace ");
```

```
    Serial.print (isgraph (' ') ?" is a" : "
is not a" );
    Serial.print ("printing character other
than a space ");
}

void loop () {
}
```

The sketch will return the following:

```
The isspace function returns:
A newline is a whitespace character
A horizontal tab is a whitespace character
% is not a whitespace character
The iscntrl function returns:
A newline is a control character
$ is not a control character
The ispunct function returns:
; is a punctuation character
Y is not a punctuation character
# is a punctuation character
The isprint function returns:
$ is a printing character
Alert is not a printing character
Space is a printing character
The isgraph function returns:
Q is a printing character other than space
Space is not a printing character other than
space
```

The *isspace* function was able to differentiate between spacing and non-spacing characters. The *iscntrl* function was able to differentiate between control and non-control characters. The *ispunct* function was able to differentiate between punctuation and non-punctuation characters. The *isprint* function was able to differentiate between printing and non-printing characters.

This marks the end of this book. You can program the Arduino board so as to come up with complex systems. An example of such a system is one that controls access to a facility. You can use Arduino to program the door that grants access to the facility. Arduino is good for hardware programming. If you are familiar with the C programming language, then it is easy for you to program the Arduino boards. The code is written in the Arduino software, which is an open source software. You can download and use this software on your system or free. The codes written in the Arduino software are known as sketches. There are a number of libraries that you need to include in your programs when programming the Arduino board. These libraries are included by the use of the "#include" keyword used in the C programming language. You can write programs that can control the Arduino LED light. Note that you can power the Arduino board from your computer or directly into the power socket, and the effect will be the same in all of these cases. Data can be sent from the computer to the Arduino board, and from the Arduino board to the computer. The RX and TX LEDs usually light to show the direction in which the data is flowing.

When programming the Arduino board, you can take advantage of the various features provided by the language including decision making statements, loops, functions, variables and others. The language also supports various data types that you can use when declaring variables. The *math.h* library comes with a number of functions that you can to perform various mathematical operations. An example of such a function is the *sqrt()* function that can help you calculate the square root of a number.

ABOUT THE AUTHOR

Daniel Bell was born in the Bronx, New York. When he was nine, he moved with his father Guy Bell to Nice in France. He received his Ph.D. degree in computer science from the University of Nice (France) in 2012. Daniel is conducting research in data management, with an emphasis on topics related to Big Data and data sharing, such as probabilistic data, data pricing, parallel data processing, data security. He spends his free time writing books on computer programming and data science, to help the absolute beginners in computer programming to code easily. He lives in Chatillon, near Paris.

A c k n o w l e d g m e n t s

Foremost, I would like to express my sincere gratitude to my family, my wife Genevieve and my son Adan for the continuous support in my everyday life, for their patience, motivation, enthusiasm. Besides my family, I would like to thank my friends and colleagues: Prof. Jule Villepreux, Hugo D. and Dr. James Rivera, for their encouragement, insightful comments, and hard questions. I thank my fellow labmates: Gang Yu, Ting Fan, Djibrilla Diallo, Juan Sanchez, for the stimulating discussions, for the sleepless nights we were working together before deadlines, and for all the fun we have had. Last but not least, I would like to thank my parents Guy Bell and Ezra Bell, for giving birth to me at the first place and supporting me spiritually throughout my life.

www.guzzlermedia.com

www.ingramcontent.com/pod-product-compliance
Lightning Source LLC
Chambersburg PA
CBHW070837070326
40690CB00009B/1588